JUN    2016

# THE TAIGA

## DISCOVER THIS FORESTED BIOME

*Philip Johansson*

**Enslow Elementary**

an imprint of

**Enslow Publishers, Inc.**

40 Industrial Road
Box 398
Berkeley Heights, NJ 07922
USA

http://www.enslow.com

Enslow Elementary, an imprint of Enslow Publishers, Inc.
Enslow Elementary® is a registered trademark of Enslow Publishers, Inc.

Originally published as *The Forested Taiga: A Web of Life* in 2004.

**Library of Congress Cataloging-in-Publication Data**

Johansson, Philip.
  The taiga : discover this forested biome / Philip Johansson.
      pages cm. — (Discover the world's biomes)
  "Originally published as The forested taiga: a web of life in 2004."
  Includes bibliographical references and index.
  ISBN 978-0-7660-6410-2
  1. Taiga ecology—Juvenile literature. I. Title. II. Series: Johansson, Philip. Discover the world's biomes.
  QH541.5.T3J64 2015
  577.3'7—dc23
                          2014027456
"Discusses the plants and animals of the taiga biome, including their roles in the food chain"—Provided by publisher.

**Future editions:**
Paperback ISBN: 978-0-7660-6411-9
EPUB ISBN: 978-0-7660-6412-6
Single-User PDF ISBN: 978-0-7660-6413-3
Multi-User PDF ISBN: 978-0-7660-6414-0

Printed in the United States of America

102014 Bang Printing, Brainerd, Minn.

10 9 8 7 6 5 4 3 2 1

**To Our Readers:** We have done our best to make sure all Internet addresses in this book were active and appropriate when we went to press. However, the author and the publisher have no control over and assume no liability for the material available on those Internet sites or on other Web sites they may link to. Any comments or suggestions can be sent by e-mail to comments@enslow.com or to the address on the back cover.

♻ Enslow Publishers, Inc., is committed to printing our books on recycled paper. The paper in every book contains 10% to 30% post-consumer waste (PCW). The cover board on the outside of each book contains 100% PCW. Our goal is to do our part to help young people and the environment, too!

**Interior Photo Credits:** © 1999 Artville, LLC, pp. 10–11. © Corel Corporation, pp. 4, 8, 14, 28, 34. Dover Publications, Inc., pp. 5, 12, 20, 26, 35. Shutterstock.com: Aleksander Bolbot, p. 13; Arto Hakola, p. 23 (hawk); Brykaylo Yuriy, p. 30; Chris Hill, p. 36; Dennis W. Donohue, pp. 25 (lynx), 42; Erni, p. 22; Ewa Studio, p. 25 (porcupine); Henry Steven, pp. 23 (pine cones), 29; Iakov Filimonov, p. 1; i-m-a-g-e, pp. 25 (aerial view of spruce trees), 27; Kichigin, p. 23 (background); Laszlo Csoma, pp. 25 (fungi), 33; MVPhoto, pp. 25 (hare), 41 (right); Panu Ruangjan, p. 25 (kingfisher); Paul Reeves Photography, pp. 25 (marten), 43; Pi-Lens, pp. 5, 9, 15; Sky Light Pictures, pp. 25 (flowers), 32; Tom Reichner, p. 41 (left); Yarygin, pp. 25 (ferns), 31; yevgeniy11, pp. 24, 25 (earthworm). © Thinkstock: Enskanto/iStock, pp. 16, 19, 25 (spruces); kjekol/iStock, p. 7; Mirosław Kijewski/iStock, pp. 23 (squirrel), 25 (squirrel), 39; photographybyJHWilliams/iStock, pp. 21, 25 (deer); photos_martYmage/iStock, pp. 40, 44; Pi-Lens/iStock, p. 18; Steve Byland/iStock, p. 39.

**Cover Credits:** Shutterstock.com: Critterbiz (Canadian lynx); owatta (Earth illustration).

Dr. Rolf Peterson is a wildlife ecologist from Michigan Technological University. He studies the ecology of moose and wolves at Isle Royale National Park, Michigan. The volunteers in Chapter 1 are from Earthwatch Institute, a non-profit organization. Earthwatch supports field science and conservation through the participation of the public. See www.earthwatch.org for more information.

# CONTENTS

Gray wolves live in the taiga forest. They hunt for moose and other animals.

# Chapter 1

# A Wolf's Dining Room

Wolves are predators of the northern forests. They live in packs, social groups that hunt together and fear little. Yet you would be very lucky to ever see a wolf, even in the taiga (TYE-guh), where they are common. This northern forest is thick and green. The trees block the sunlight and make it hard to see anything along the trail. And wolves, with their keen sense of smell and eyesight, can easily avoid humans.

**Dr. Rolf Peterson is a biologist. He studies wolves in Isle Royale National Park, Michigan, in the middle of Lake Superior. He has to hike through the woods for hours, far from any trail, to find signs of wolves.**

**Peterson and two volunteers have been walking through the thick forest all morning. The land is rugged. The summer day is hot, and the forest smells of fir trees. Blackflies and mosquitoes are thick in the still air. "Hey, here's something," a volunteer assistant finally says. The assistant pushes some fir branches out of the way and bends over. He picks up a bone about as long as his forearm. It is the jawbone of a moose.**

## A Winter's Kill

"This is one of the unlucky ones," says Peterson. He says that the jawbone is from an old moose. He can tell from its size and the wear on its teeth. The moose was probably killed by wolves last winter. "It might have been trapped in this thick stand of fir trees," says Peterson.

Wolves are careful hunters, usually only chasing moose that are sick or old. They know better than to stalk a healthy adult, which can stand six and a half feet (two meters) tall and

*Wolves are top predators in the food chain. This wolf has found its next meal.*

weigh almost 1,000 pounds (455 kilograms). When wolves are successful, there is enough moose meat to feed a large pack.

"Last winter was about as good as it gets for a wolf," says Peterson. "With heavy snow cover, wolves on the island had an easy time catching prey. The deep snow made traveling tough for moose. Wolves had the advantage."

Not every winter is the same in the northern forests like those on Isle Royale. Some winters are mild with little snowfall. Then, moose are better able to defend themselves against wolves.

## Learning From Wolves

After studying the moose's jawbone, the assistant puts it into a bag and labels it. Peterson searches the ground for more bones from the animal. They collect a skull and a leg bone showing the

*A pack of wolves stands at the edge of the forest.*

scratches from a gnawing wolf. Then they push on through the forest for several more miles. The bones may be the only sign of a moose kill they find that day, but they are an important piece of a puzzle.

Peterson has been studying moose and wolves here for more than thirty years. He has seen the numbers of wolves and moose go up and down. Peterson is watching how the wolf (a predator) and the moose (its prey) live together. Learning more about wolves and their prey could help scientists understand the taiga better.

# WHAT IS A BIOME?

The taiga is one kind of biome. A biome is a large region of Earth where certain plants and animals live. They survive there because they are well suited to the plants and climate found in that area. The climate is a result of the temperatures and amounts of rainfall that usually occur during a year.

Each biome has plants that may not be found in other biomes. Trees grow in forests, but not in deserts. Cacti grow in deserts, but not in grasslands. The animals that eat these plants add to the living communities of a biome. Exploring biomes is a good way to understand how these communities work. In this book, you will learn about the taiga biome and the plants and animals that live there.

## LEGEND

- Tundra
- Taiga
- Temperate forest
- Grassland
- Desert
- Rain forest
- Chaparral
- Mountain zone
- Polar ice

*Biomes of the World*

# Chapter 2

# The Taiga Biome

The taiga biome is a land of deep, dark evergreen forests. It is a wide section of forests stretching through northern Europe, Asia, and North America. Taiga is the largest land biome, making up one third of all the forests on Earth. It circles the globe between the tundra in the far north and the warmer, temperate forests to the south. Taiga can also be found high in the mountains of warmer areas. The word *taiga* comes from the Russian word for "forest" because so much of Russia is covered with this biome. Another name for this biome is *boreal forest*. *Boreal* refers to the cold, northern land where the forest is found.

*The dark green taiga is filled with different plants.*

*Winter temperatures can be below freezing for six months.*

## Taiga Weather

There is a wide range of temperatures in the taiga between winter and summer. The taiga has long, severe winters. For up to six months, the temperatures are below freezing (32 degrees Fahrenheit, or 0 degrees Celsius). Winter nights can get as cold as –65 degrees Fahrenheit (–54 degrees Celsius). The warmest winter days may be only 30 degrees Fahrenheit (–1 degree Celsius).

Summers in the taiga are short. There may be fewer than three months without frost on the ground. This is the only time when delicate plants are able to grow on the forest floor.

Although the summers are short, temperatures are pleasant. Summer days may warm up to 90 degrees Fahrenheit (32 degrees Celsius). Nights cool down to 40 degrees Fahrenheit (4 degrees Celsius), which is just above freezing. Many plants and animals thrive in the taiga during the summer.

*Although winter lasts for many months, the taiga has all four seasons. This photograph shows the taiga in autumn.*

The seasons are not equal in length, as they are in temperate forests closer to the equator. Spring and autumn in the taiga are so short, they go by almost without notice. Temperatures during these times are between those of winter and summer.

*Taiga trees can grow as tall as 100 feet (30 meters).*

## A Thirsty Forest

Although it looks lush and green, the taiga does not get as much precipitation as most other forests. It gets only as much rain and snow as most grasslands, which is not a lot. It receives between 12 and 33 inches (30 and 84 centimeters) of precipitation throughout the year. Most of that moisture falls during the summer. But the taiga is very good at keeping this water in the forest.

Because it is so far north, the sunlight in the taiga is not as strong as it is in other forests. Without the direct heat of the sun, very little water evaporates from the forest. The result is a surprisingly humid environment, even with the lack of rain. Taiga trees grow tall, up to 100 feet (30 meters), using the abundant water trapped in the soil. Other plants thrive on the damp forest floor.

## Young Soil

There is only a thin layer of soil in the taiga. This soil is poor in nutrients. (Nutrients are chemicals that plants and animals need to live and grow.) One reason for these soil conditions is that only a few thousand years ago, the region was covered with glaciers. That sounds like a long time, but it is really a short time for building soil on bare rock. There has not been time for deep soils to develop.

The thin taiga soil comes from rotting leaves and wood. But taiga forests do not produce a lot of falling leaves. That is because the evergreen trees of the taiga hold on to most of their needles. The needles they do drop are tough and do not break down easily into soil.

Dead plants and animals decay very slowly in the cold taiga climate. Bacteria, insects, worms, fungi, and other soil life work to break down dead plants and animals. They release nutrients that plants can use. But the bacteria work very slowly in the cold soil, so there are few nutrients present for the plants. Taiga plants are especially suited to grow in these soils and in the shady conditions found on the forest floor.

*The taiga has a very thin layer of soil. One reason is that there has not yet been enough time for soil to build up.*

# TAIGA FACTS

**Temperatures vary:** Winters are cold, as low as –65 degrees Fahrenheit (–54 degrees Celsius). Summers are warm, ranging up to 90 degrees Fahrenheit (32 degrees Celsius).

**Low precipitation:** Most precipitation falls as summer rain.

**Moist conditions under tall trees.**

**Short growing season:** Plants grow for about only three months of the year.

**Thin soil:** The soil is young, only a few thousand years old, so it is not deep.

**Slow rate of decay:** Soil animals and fungi that break down dead plants and animals move slowly in the cold soil.

# Chapter 3

# Biome Communities

The taiga is made up of communities of plants and animals, just like every other biome. Communities are the groups of living things found together in a place. In a community, some plants and animals depend on others. Each plant and animal has a role in the community.

## Plants and Energy

Plants in a community trap energy from sunlight. They use the sun's energy to make sugar from carbon dioxide (a gas in the air) and the water from the soil. They later use the energy in the sugars to build new leaves, stems, roots, and flowers.

Some animals, such as caterpillars, red squirrels, and deer, eat these plants. Animals that eat only plants are called herbivores. Herbivores get their energy from plants. Other animals, called carnivores, eat herbivores. Woodpeckers and wolves are carnivores. Carnivores get their energy from the meat of other animals. Omnivores, such as sparrows, eat both plants and animals.

When plants and animals die, soil animals and fungi get to work. They help break down the dead plants and animals. This releases nutrients back into the soil. Earthworms, beetles, fungi, microbes, and other soil life step in to do this job. These animals are called decomposers.

*A mule deer is one of the plant eaters of the taiga biome.*

*The northern three-toed woodpecker is a carnivore. It eats the meat of other animals, like grubs and insects it finds in trees.*

## The Food Web

The flow of energy from the sun to plants to herbivores to carnivores follows a pattern called a food web. A bit like a spider's web, the food web connects the plants and animals of a community, showing who eats whom. For example, red squirrels eat seeds from a pinecone. Cooper's hawks eat red squirrels. When a hawk dies, bacteria and worms feast on the dead animal.

# SUNLIGHT

USED BY

PLANTS ～～～ HEAT LOSS

EATEN BY

HERBIVORES ～～～ HEAT LOSS

EATEN BY

CARNIVORES ～～～ HEAT LOSS

SOIL LIFE
(decomposers)

At each stage in the flow of energy through the taiga community, some energy is lost as heat.

Plants and animals pass energy through the community. At each stage of the food web, some energy is lost as the plants and animals use it to live. Plants must trap more energy from the sun to keep themselves and the animals in the community alive.

*Soil animals, such as this earthworm, break down dead plants and animals.*

## Learning From Biomes

Exploring biomes like the taiga is a good way to learn how all living communities work. By looking at the plants and animals in any biome, you may see how some of them interact with each other. If you take any plant or animal away, it could change how the community works.

# SOME PLANTS AND ANIMALS IN THE
# TAIGA FOOD WEB

| PLANTS | HERBIVORES | CARNIVORES |
|---|---|---|
| Eaten by → | Eaten by → | |

**PLANTS**

Firs

Spruces

Pines

Sedges

Ferns

Mosses

Wildflowers

Blueberries

Lichens

**HERBIVORES**

Red Squirrels

Deer

Moose

Elk

Porcupines

Snowshoe Hares

Grubs

Insects

**CARNIVORES**

Lynx

Cooper's Hawks

Wolves

Woodpeckers

Kingfishers

Thrushes

Martens

## SOIL LIFE

Worms          Beetles          Bacteria          Fungi

# Chapter 4

# Taiga Plants

If you were flying over the taiga in an airplane, the forest would look like a sea of dark green. Taiga trees grow close together. Little sunlight gets through to the forest floor because the tops of many of the tall trees touch each other. They form a canopy over the forest floor. The trees trap energy from the sun. They are the first step in the flow of energy through the taiga community. Unlike the variety in other forest biomes, the kinds of trees found in the taiga are few. Varieties of evergreens—spruce, fir, pine, and cedar—make up most of

*Spruce trees form a blanket of green in Canada.*

the forest. From a distance, it is difficult to tell many
of these trees apart because they have similar forms.
Other trees, such as aspen and birch, grow among them
in places. Their leaves are a brighter green, and they let
more light through to the forest floor. These trees are
deciduous. They lose their leaves every autumn.

Evergreen spruce trees and deciduous aspen trees grow in the taiga. The aspen lose their leaves in the autumn.

Most of the trees of the taiga carry their seeds in cones, like the pinecones found under pine trees. These trees are called conifers, meaning "cone-bearing."

The cones on taiga trees are pollinated by the wind. The wind carries the pollen from one tree to the cones of another. Then seeds can grow in the cone. For this reason it is helpful that the trees grow close together.

## The Shape of Taiga Trees

The leaves of taiga conifers are needlelike. They range from the short, flat needles of fir to the long, narrow needles of pines. Their needle shape helps them hold water. They have less surface area than broad, flat leaves, so there is less area from which to lose water. This is especially important in the dry, cold winter, when the frozen ground prevents the trees from taking up more water.

*The needles of this pine tree are long and narrow. The pinecone contains the tree's seeds.*

*Spruce trees have a pyramid shape. The shape helps the snow fall off the trees. This way, the limbs are less likely to break from the weight of the snow.*

Conifer trees of the taiga share many other features as well. They are evergreens. Their needles stay green through the winter. This allows them to start trapping energy from sunlight right away in the spring. They do not have to wait to grow new leaves the way that deciduous trees do. They also save energy by not dropping their needles every fall. Some spruces have been known to keep their needles for fifteen years.

Conifer needles have a thick, waxy coating that protects them from the drying winds. The coating also keeps the inside of the needle from freezing in the chill of winter.

Conifer trees have a narrow cone shape that helps them shed snow in the winter. Their branches droop down rather than reaching up like other trees. Snow slides off the branches before the snow's weight can break them.

## Under the Canopy

Beneath the thick taiga treetops, other plants are sometimes rare. Where they can find a bit of sunlight, ferns and mosses thrive. Mushrooms grow on fallen trees and help turn the wood into soil. Low-growing, ancient plants called club mosses may create a carpet over large areas. Sedges, which are like sharp grasses, grow in damper places. In openings where trees have blown down, shrubs such as blackberry may spring up.

*When sunlight can reach the forest floor, ferns and mosses grow. Fallen trees can eventually break down into soil.*

Wildflowers can be found scattered on the forest floor, especially under areas of deciduous trees. These wildflowers attract insects during the short summer. Drooping trilliums and showy ladyslippers are some of the first, followed by Canada mayflowers and trout lilies. In autumn, there are blue and white asters to brighten up the dark ground.

Like the small variety of taiga trees, there is a small variety of plants on the forest floor. The severe winter environment allows only a few types of plants to grow here. Many of the plants are perennials, which means they come back every summer from

*Among a patch of recently burned trees, a field of fireweed plants grow.*

the same root. These include blueberries, partridgeberries, snowberries, and cranberries. They survive under the snow to grow again during the short summer.

## Trunks of Energy

Most of the energy in the taiga biome is locked in the trees that cover the land. The trees use the sun's energy to change nutrients from the air and soil into their massive trunks, roots, branches, and leaves. Most of these nutrients are not available to other plants and animals in the forest until the tree dies. This may take two or three hundred years.

*Fungi grow on a dead tree.*

Wildfires are helpful in taiga forests. When wildfires burn, they release the nutrients locked up in the trees. They also open up areas of the forest for new growth. Many of the deciduous trees found in the taiga grow in recently burned areas. They provide important habitat for wildflowers as well as animals such as deer and beavers.

Once a forest tree dies, insects, mushrooms, and microbes start to work. They slowly break down the tree into material for the rest of the forest food web. These nutrients can be used to help more plants grow.

# TAIGA PLANTS

**Mostly conifer trees:** Evergreen trees, including fir, spruce, pine, and cedar, bear their seeds in cones.

**Very few species of trees compared to other kinds of forests.**

**Energy locked in trees:** Trees do not release the energy until they die.

**Cone-shaped trees:** Overall shape and downward-sloping branches let snow slide off.

**Many mosses, mushrooms, and ferns.**

**Evergreen needles:** Narrow, needle-shaped leaves help to keep water from being lost from trees. Waxy coating also helps save water and prevents freezing.

**Dark forest floor:** Thick canopy lets little sunlight through to forest floor, which may be bare of plants.

**Many perennial plants:** Blueberries, partridgeberries, and other perennials survive under the winter snow to grow again each summer.

# Chapter 5

# Taiga Animals

Using the energy and nutrients stored in taiga plants, taiga animals continue the food web of this biome. Like the trees of the taiga, there are fewer kinds of animals living in the taiga than in other forest biomes. The harsh winter prevents some animals from living here.

There is plenty of plant food during the summer, but that is less than one hundred days of the year. In the winter, animals must be able to live with a lack of food, as

35

well as with severe temperatures. Taiga animals have special adaptations to survive these conditions and to make the most of the resources in the taiga forest.

## Small Taiga Creatures

Reptiles and amphibians are rare in the taiga. Because they need sunlight to help keep themselves warm, they cannot survive the long, cold winters. Only a handful of hardy salamanders and frogs can survive here, such as the redback salamander and the wood frog. They spend the winter nestled under the soil, then come out in the spring to feast on insects. They lay their eggs in ponds and shallow pools.

*Wood frogs live in the taiga.*

Insects are plentiful in the summer. They survive the winter by going dormant, which is like going into a deep sleep. Some insects spend the winter as adults. Others lay eggs in the autumn and die, leaving their next generation to overwinter as eggs or grubs. Many insects need pools of water or streams of melted snow for part of their life cycle. They lay their eggs in the water, and their young develop there in the spring.

Hordes of mosquitoes, blackflies, and deerflies thrive in the taiga summer. These carnivores fill the still, humid air beneath the forest canopy with their humming and buzzing. Caterpillars, beetles, and other insects live in the forest canopy or on the bark of trees. These plant-eating insects continue the flow of energy from the plants they eat to larger animals, such as birds.

## Taiga Birds

Thousands of forest birds feast on the clouds of insects that swarm in the spring. Most birds migrate to warmer climates to avoid the winter's food shortage. They return in the spring to breed and raise their young.

Warblers in a rainbow of colors and grosbeaks in bold patterns decorate the dark branches of the evergreens. Thrushes with speckled breasts flit along the forest floor. In the early summer, the forest is filled with their tuneful songs. Each male bird uses a distinctive song to try to attract a mate and to defend its territory.

A few birds manage to live in the taiga through the harsh winter. These have thick, warm layers of downy feathers to ward off the cold. Gray jays and chickadees hide food in tree cavities and under bark to last them through the winter. Woodpeckers find grubs and insects waiting out the winter inside trees.

Crossbills have special beaks for prying the stubborn seeds out of conifer cones.

Each of these forest birds may be eaten by various small predators. Predators are the next level in the food web. Cooper's hawks swoop through the forest to prey on birds in flight. Weasels stalk thrushes and other birds close to the ground. Ravens live on animals that have died.

*Bright yellow warblers stand out in the evergreen trees of the taiga.*

## Taiga Mammals

Most mammals of the taiga are active through the winter. Their winter coats are thick and fluffy to keep their body heat in. Eating keeps them warm, so they need to constantly search for food.

Red squirrels keep busy in the treetops. They strip down the abundant cones for their seeds, which are high in energy. Squirrels are specially adapted to live in the treetops, traveling through the forest by jumping from tree to tree. They have sharp claws for climbing and a bushy tail to help them balance on branches. Like many forest animals, they store food for the cold winter, when food is hard to find.

Deer, moose, caribou, and elk remain active in the winter, too. They find shelter from the deep snow under thick groves of evergreens. A few mammals, like black bears, will sleep through the winter. Although they do not store food, they store energy in the form of body fat to survive the winter months. Others, like raccoons and chipmunks, will spend the coldest times curled up in a nest with stored food. They will come out to eat when the weather is not too severe or the snow too deep.

*A red squirrel's bushy tail helps it balance on the branches of tall taiga trees.*

*Woodland caribou stay active in the winter. They seek cover under groups of evergreen trees.*

Snowshoe hares are specially adapted to winter. They have large hind feet that keep them from sinking in the deep snow. Their thick, warm coats turn white in the winter to match the snow, when they survive on buds and twigs. In the summer, their coats turn brown to blend in with the forest floor. This seasonal color change helps protect snowshoe hares from predators because they are hard to see in their surroundings.

## Predators of the Taiga

One of the most eager hunters of snowshoe hares is the lynx, a larger relative of the bobcat. Lynx have large paws for walking on the snow.

Some predators at the top of the taiga food web may focus on other prey. Fishers—large, tree-climbing members of the weasel family—specialize in hunting porcupines. Martens, a slightly smaller member of the weasel family, live almost completely on squirrels. Other predators are less picky. Wolverines are the largest members of the weasel family. They have a reputation for eating anything that does not move out of their way.

The wolves studied by Dr. Rolf Peterson are top predators in the taiga. They are the only wild animals able to kill a moose. They also eat many small mammals, such as hares and beavers.

*A snowshoe hare has a brown coat in the summer and a white coat in the winter to help it hide from predators.*

*The lynx is one of the predators of the taiga. Its enormous padded paws help it move in the snow.*

*A pine marten comes out of its den to hunt squirrels.*

To keep a healthy food web in the taiga biome, it is important to help predators like wolves survive.

The taiga is a huge forest biome, with many distinctive features. A special community of taiga plants and animals lives here, surviving cold winters and short summers. These plants and animals are the heart of the taiga food web. Energy flows through them to fill this forest with life.

# ANIMAL FACTS

Fur or feathers keep in body heat.

Large feet act like snowshoes to help animals walk on top of the snow.

Feast or famine: Most animals find more food in the summer than the winter. Most birds fly south to find more food. Many animals store food in nests, or they store energy in the form of fat.

Eating cones: Some animals have special adaptations for eating the seeds out of cones.

Sleeping through winter: Bears sleep through most of the winter, living off stored fat. Raccoons and chipmunks sleep through the coldest spells, coming out to feed on warmer winter days.

Climbing trees: Many mammals with sharp claws climb trees for food and safety.

Insects overwinter: Some adult insects wait out the cold winter buried underground. Others wait in the form of eggs or pupae. They emerge to continue their life cycle in the short taiga summer.

# WORDS TO KNOW

**ADAPTATION**—A trait of a plant or animal that helps it survive the conditions where it lives.

**BIOME**—An area of the earth defined by the kinds of plants that live there.

**BOREAL**—Referring to things in the north.

**CANOPY**—The top of a tree or trees where most of the leafy branches are.

**CARNIVORE**—An animal that eats other animals.

**CLIMATE**—The average weather conditions in an area, usually measured over years. It includes temperature, precipitation, and wind speeds.

**COMMUNITY**—The collection of plants and animals living and interacting in an area.

**CONIFER**—A kind of tree that has its seeds in cones, including pines, firs, spruces, and hemlocks.

**DECAY**—The breakdown of dead plants or animals into nutrients by bacteria, fungi, and other living things.

**DECIDUOUS**—Trees that drop their leaves in the autumn and grow new ones in the spring.

**EVERGREEN**—A plant that keeps its green leaves throughout the year.

**FOOD WEB**—The relationships between living things that allow the transfer of energy and nutrients from plants to herbivores to carnivores to decomposers.

**HERBIVORE**—An animal that eats plants.

**MICROBE**—A very simple, very small organism made of a single cell. Some microbes help decompose dead animals and plants. There are many kinds of microbes, and there are many millions of microbes in a spoonful of soil.

**MIGRATE**—To travel from one place to another on a regular schedule.

**NUTRIENTS**—The chemicals that plants need in order to live and grow.

**OMNIVORE**—An animal that eats both plants and other animals.

**PERENNIAL**—A plant that stores nutrients in its roots in order to survive through the winter. The same plant blooms every year from the root rather than from a seed.

**POLLINATE**—To transfer pollen from one flower to another, by wind or by animals such as bees and flies. Pollination is necessary for plants to make seeds and reproduce.

**PRECIPITATION**—Water in the form of rain, snow, or fog.

**PREDATOR**—An animal that hunts other animals for food.

**PREY**—An animal that is hunted by another for food. Also, to kill and eat another animal.

**TEMPERATE**—Moderate, not extreme, referring to the climate of temperate forests.

# LEARN MORE

Day, Trevor. *Taiga.* Chicago, Ill.: Heinemann-Raintree, 2011.

Johnson, Rebecca L. *A Walk in the Boreal Forest.* Minneapolis, Minn.: The Lerner Publishing Group, 2000.

Kaplan, Elizabeth. *Taiga.* Tarrytown, N.Y.: Marshall Cavendish Corp., 1996.

Rutten, Joshua. *Forests.* Chanhassen, Minn.: The Child's World, Inc., 1998.

Simon, Seymour. *Wildfires.* New York: HarperCollins, 1996.

# INDEX